FUCK
NICOTINE

COLORING BOOK
Quit Smoking
in 21 days

In the same collection

FUCK ADDICTION
Sobriety
Coloring Journal

FUCK BINGE EATING
Inspiring coloring book
for ED Recovery

Scan to watch
on amazon.com

A COLORING BOOK TO QUIT SMOKING ?

Nicotine patch, hypnosis, relaxation, switching to electronic cigarettes, gradual cessation ... you've tried it all.

But nothing works!

The problem with most methods to quit smoking is that they don't take the problem head on.

Your enemy is not cigarettes, but nicotine.
It's the nicotine that lies to your brain and makes you want to smoke.
It's the nicotine that makes you think life is cooler with cigarettes.
It's what makes you feel relaxed after smoking.

To get cigarettes out of your life, cut out nicotine.
You can't fight nicotine with a nicotine patch.
Nor with an electronic cigarette.

You fight nicotine head-on, in a duel, in single combat.
And to win a fight, there's nothing like knowing your enemy.

The luck of the story is that nicotine stays in your body for about 21 days.
It's scientific!

To win the fight against nicotine, just stay off it for 21 days.
Nothing could be simpler.
If you haven't smoked in 21 days, then you will be a non-smoker.

Simple? Yes.

Easy? No !

UNDERSTAND YOUR ENNEMI :
THE NICOTINE

Nicotine is a little monster inside you.

A monster that shows its nose every time you wake up.
Every time you go outside in the morning.
Every time you see that friend.
Every time you finish your job.
Every time you smell coffee.

You probably have your own smoking rituals.

The important thing is to identify them, and to realize when nicotine is trying to trick you.
Nicotine is sneaky and can easily lie to you.

It's just a matter of recognizing it, and saying no...

HOW TO SAY NO ?

This book is not a miracle method to quit smoking.

It will simply be your companion for 21 days every time nicotine tries to fool you.

As soon as you feel like smoking, color it in!

One coloring a day for 21 days to help you get through the hard times of craving, when nicotine will push you to light a new cigarette.

When this happens, start, continue or finish a coloring session started earlier.

Color in, and the craving will disappear on its own.

Moments of craving will become less and less regular and difficult to overcome over the 21 days, until they completely disappear.

To motivate you, to help you identify them and anticipate them as well as possible, each daily coloring is accompanied by a diary to be filled in.

Every time you feel like lighting a cigarette, write it down!
- What time is it?
- What are you doing?
- Who are you?
- How do you feel?

Cigarettes	Craving	What I was doing	Who was I with	Mood
1				
2				
3				
4				
5				
6				
7				
8				
9				
10				
11				
12				
13				
14				
15				
16				
17				
18				
19				
20				

You have decided to start the fight.

From today, you start a 21-day fight.

For 21 days, do not touch nicotine anymore, and help yourself with this book to better support the fight.

Simple: yes. Easy? no.
Possible? yes!

In 21 days, you will be a non-smoker...

And will finally be able to live a full and relaxed life even...

... without nicotine.

Day 1

Date / /

_____

_____

_____

_____

Today's positive quote

"
_____
                                                "
_____

Cigarettes	Craving	What I was doing	Who was I with	Mood
1				
2				
3				
4				
5				
6				
7				
8				
9				
10				
11				
12				
13				
14				
15				
16				
17				
18				
19				
20				

My wins for today are

_____

_____

_____

Today's main difficulties were

_____

_____

_____

My goals for tomorrow

_____

_____

_____

Notes

_____

_____

_____

Day 2

Date / /

What I am grateful for today

_____

_____

_____

_____

Today's positive quote

"

_____

"

_____

Cigarettes	Craving	What I was doing	Who was I with	Mood
1				
2				
3				
4				
5				
6				
7				
8				
9				
10				
11				
12				
13				
14				
15				
16				
17				
18				
19				
20				

My wins for today are

_____

_____

_____

_____

Today's main difficulties were

_____

_____

_____

_____

My goals for tomorrow

_____

_____

_____

_____

Notes

_____

_____

_____

Day 3

Date / /

What I am grateful for today

_____

_____

_____

_____

Today's positive quote

"

_____

"

_____

Cigarettes	Craving	What I was doing	Who was I with	Mood
1				
2				
3				
4				
5				
6				
7				
8				
9				
10				
11				
12				
13				
14				
15				
16				
17				
18				
19				
20				

My wins for today are

_____

_____

_____

_____

Today's main difficulties were

_____

_____

_____

_____

My goals for tomorrow

_____

_____

_____

_____

Notes

_____

_____

_____

Day 4

Date / /

What I am grateful for today

_____

_____

_____

_____

Today's positive quote

"

_____

"

_____

Cigarettes	Craving	What I was doing	Who was I with	Mood
1				
2				
3				
4				
5				
6				
7				
8				
9				
10				
11				
12				
13				
14				
15				
16				
17				
18				
19				
20				

My wins for today are

_____

_____

_____

_____

Today's main difficulties were

_____

_____

_____

_____

My goals for tomorrow

_____

_____

_____

_____

Notes

_____

_____

_____

Day 5

What I am grateful for today

_____

_____

_____

_____

Today's positive quote

"

_____

"

_____

Cigarettes	Craving	What I was doing	Who was I with	Mood
1				
2				
3				
4				
5				
6				
7				
8				
9				
10				
11				
12				
13				
14				
15				
16				
17				
18				
19				
20				

My wins for today are

_____

_____

_____

_____

Today's main difficulties were

_____

_____

_____

_____

My goals for tomorrow

_____

_____

_____

_____

Notes

_____

_____

_____

Day 6

Date / /

What I am grateful for today

_____

_____

_____

_____

Today's positive quote

"

_____

"

_____

Cigarettes	Craving	What I was doing	Who was I with	Mood
1				
2				
3				
4				
5				
6				
7				
8				
9				
10				
11				
12				
13				
14				
15				
16				
17				
18				
19				
20				

My wins for today are

_____

_____

_____

_____

Today's main difficulties were

_____

_____

_____

_____

My goals for tomorrow

_____

_____

_____

_____

Notes

_____

_____

_____

DON'T THINK of it as QUITTING, think of it AS winning

Day 7

What I am grateful for today

_____

_____

_____

_____

Today's positive quote

"

_____

_____
"

Cigarettes	Craving	What I was doing	Who was I with	Mood
1				
2				
3				
4				
5				
6				
7				
8				
9				
10				
11				
12				
13				
14				
15				
16				
17				
18				
19				
20				

My wins for today are

_____

_____

_____

_____

Today's main difficulties were

_____

_____

_____

_____

My goals for tomorrow

_____

_____

_____

_____

Notes

_____

_____

_____

Day 8

Date / /

_____

_____

_____

_____

Today's positive quote

"

_____

"

_____

Cigarettes	Craving	What I was doing	Who was I with	Mood
1				
2				
3				
4				
5				
6				
7				
8				
9				
10				
11				
12				
13				
14				
15				
16				
17				
18				
19				
20				

My wins for today are

_____

_____

_____

_____

Today's main difficulties were

_____

_____

_____

_____

My goals for tomorrow

_____

_____

_____

_____

Notes

_____

_____

_____

Day 9

Date / /

_____

_____

_____

_____

Today's positive quote

"

_____
                                            "
_____

Cigarettes	Craving	What I was doing	Who was I with	Mood
1				
2				
3				
4				
5				
6				
7				
8				
9				
10				
11				
12				
13				
14				
15				
16				
17				
18				
19				
20				

My wins for today are

_____

_____

_____

_____

Today's main difficulties were

_____

_____

_____

_____

My goals for tomorrow

_____

_____

_____

_____

Notes

_____

_____

_____

Day 10

Date / /

What I am grateful for today

_____

_____

_____

_____

Today's positive quote

"

_____

"

_____

Cigarettes	Craving	What I was doing	Who was I with	Mood
1				
2				
3				
4				
5				
6				
7				
8				
9				
10				
11				
12				
13				
14				
15				
16				
17				
18				
19				
20				

My wins for today are

_____

_____

_____

Today's main difficulties were

_____

_____

_____

My goals for tomorrow

_____

_____

_____

Notes

_____

_____

Day 11

What I am grateful for today

_____

_____

_____

_____

Today's positive quote

"

_____

"

_____

Cigarettes	Craving	What I was doing	Who was I with	Mood
1				
2				
3				
4				
5				
6				
7				
8				
9				
10				
11				
12				
13				
14				
15				
16				
17				
18				
19				
20				

My wins for today are

_____

_____

_____

_____

Today's main difficulties were

_____

_____

_____

_____

My goals for tomorrow

_____

_____

_____

_____

Notes

_____

_____

_____

Day 12

Date / /

_____

_____

_____

_____

Today's positive quote

"

_____

"

_____

Cigarettes	Craving	What I was doing	Who was I with	Mood
1				
2				
3				
4				
5				
6				
7				
8				
9				
10				
11				
12				
13				
14				
15				
16				
17				
18				
19				
20				

My wins for today are

_____

_____

_____

_____

Today's main difficulties were

_____

_____

_____

_____

My goals for tomorrow

_____

_____

_____

_____

Notes

_____

_____

_____

Day 13

Date / /

_____

_____

_____

_____

Today's positive quote

"

_____

"

_____

Cigarettes	Craving	What I was doing	Who was I with	Mood
1				
2				
3				
4				
5				
6				
7				
8				
9				
10				
11				
12				
13				
14				
15				
16				
17				
18				
19				
20				

My wins for today are

_____

_____

_____

_____

Today's main difficulties were

_____

_____

_____

_____

My goals for tomorrow

_____

_____

_____

_____

Notes

_____

_____

_____

Day 14

Date / /

What I am grateful for today

_____

_____

_____

_____

Today's positive quote

"

_____

                                        "

_____

Cigarettes	Craving	What I was doing	Who was I with	Mood
1				
2				
3				
4				
5				
6				
7				
8				
9				
10				
11				
12				
13				
14				
15				
16				
17				
18				
19				
20				

My wins for today are

_____

_____

_____

_____

Today's main difficulties were

_____

_____

_____

_____

My goals for tomorrow

_____

_____

_____

_____

Notes

_____

_____

_____

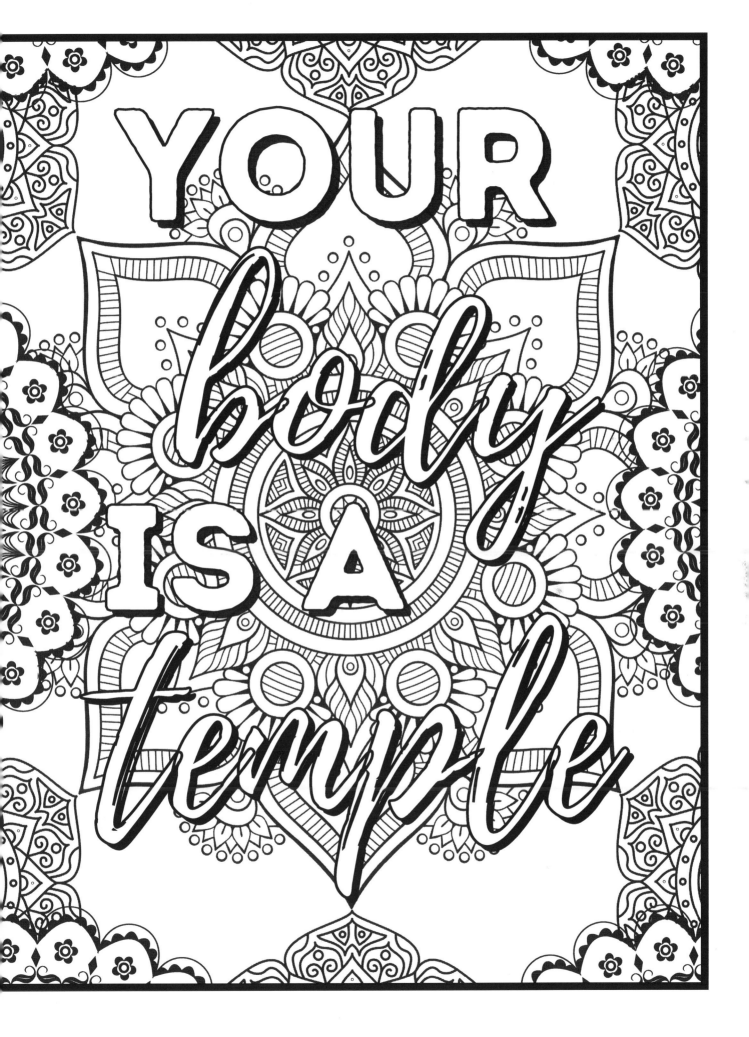

Day 15

Date / /

What I am grateful for today

_____

_____

_____

_____

Today's positive quote

"

_____

"

_____

Cigarettes	Craving	What I was doing	Who was I with	Mood
1				
2				
3				
4				
5				
6				
7				
8				
9				
10				
11				
12				
13				
14				
15				
16				
17				
18				
19				
20				

My wins for today are

_____

_____

_____

_____

Today's main difficulties were

_____

_____

_____

_____

My goals for tomorrow

_____

_____

_____

_____

Notes

_____

_____

Day 16

Date / /

What I am grateful for today

_____

_____

_____

_____

Today's positive quote

"

_____

"

_____

Cigarettes	Craving	What I was doing	Who was I with	Mood
1				
2				
3				
4				
5				
6				
7				
8				
9				
10				
11				
12				
13				
14				
15				
16				
17				
18				
19				
20				

My wins for today are

_____

_____

_____

_____

Today's main difficulties were

_____

_____

_____

_____

My goals for tomorrow

_____

_____

_____

_____

Notes

_____

_____

_____

Day 17

Date / /

_____

_____

_____

_____

Today's positive quote

"

_____

"

_____

Cigarettes	Craving	What I was doing	Who was I with	Mood
1				
2				
3				
4				
5				
6				
7				
8				
9				
10				
11				
12				
13				
14				
15				
16				
17				
18				
19				
20				

My wins for today are

_____

_____

_____

_____

Today's main difficulties were

_____

_____

_____

_____

My goals for tomorrow

_____

_____

_____

_____

Notes

_____

_____

_____

Day 18

Date / /

What I am grateful for today

_____

_____

_____

_____

Today's positive quote

"

_____

"

_____

Cigarettes	Craving	What I was doing	Who was I with	Mood
1				
2				
3				
4				
5				
6				
7				
8				
9				
10				
11				
12				
13				
14				
15				
16				
17				
18				
19				
20				

My wins for today are

_____

_____

_____

_____

Today's main difficulties were

_____

_____

_____

_____

My goals for tomorrow

_____

_____

_____

_____

Notes

_____

_____

_____

Day 19

What I am grateful for today

_____

_____

_____

_____

Today's positive quote

"

_____

"

_____

Cigarettes	Craving	What I was doing	Who was I with	Mood
1				
2				
3				
4				
5				
6				
7				
8				
9				
10				
11				
12				
13				
14				
15				
16				
17				
18				
19				
20				

My wins for today are

_____

_____

_____

_____

Today's main difficulties were

_____

_____

_____

_____

My goals for tomorrow

_____

_____

_____

_____

Notes

_____

_____

_____

Day 20

What I am grateful for today

_____

_____

_____

_____

Today's positive quote

"

_____

"

_____

Cigarettes	Craving	What I was doing	Who was I with	Mood
1				
2				
3				
4				
5				
6				
7				
8				
9				
10				
11				
12				
13				
14				
15				
16				
17				
18				
19				
20				

My wins for today are

_____

_____

_____

Today's main difficulties were

_____

_____

_____

My goals for tomorrow

_____

_____

_____

Notes

_____

_____

Day 21

Date / /

What I am grateful for today

Today's positive quote

"

"

Cigarettes	Craving	What I was doing	Who was I with	Mood
1				
2				
3				
4				
5				
6				
7				
8				
9				
10				
11				
12				
13				
14				
15				
16				
17				
18				
19				
20				

My wins for today are

_____

_____

_____

_____

Today's main difficulties were

_____

_____

_____

_____

My goals for tomorrow

_____

_____

_____

_____

Notes

_____

_____

_____

Printed in Great Britain
by Amazon